AN AMAZING CIRCUS OF PHONOGRAMS

ACT 1

By Mary Jo Nyssen • Illustrated by Mike Motz

I dedicate this book to all of my loving daughters
Charlene, Michelle, Joyce, Beth Ann, Kristi
and my devoted husband Richard
who have all been so supportive of my writing.

ISBN: 0692250158
ISBN 13: 9780692250150
Library of Congress Control Number: 2015900113
MOM-BA-BOOKS
Salem, OR

Introduction to the reader of

In my first book, *A Colorful Journey Through the Land of Talking Letters*, I introduced the first 26 letters of the alphabet (26 phonograms) and their sounds. The remaining 44 phonograms of the 70 total phonograms have more than one letter in their makeup. This book (Act One) introduces 22 of these 44 phonograms. The remaining 22 phonograms will be presented in my third book (Act Two.)

The 22 phonograms included in Act One are the five differently spelled **"er"** sounds – **er, ir, ur, ear,** and **wor,** and the other seventeen are **sh, ee, th, ay, ai, ow, ou, oa, oy, oi, aw, au, ew, ui, oo, ch** and **ea.**

Each phonogram which is being presented will be color highlighted in the stories. Those phonograms that have only one sound will be purple. The phonograms that have more than one sound will be highlighted as follows: the first will be green, the second red, the third blue, the forth orange, and the fifth yellow.

Once Children learn the first 26 phonograms or letters of the alphabet and their sounds it is much easier to start teaching the other 44 phonograms. Knowing these 70 phonograms will help a child spell and read most words proficiently at an early age.

Come boys and girls to the big top show
Where you will see and hear things you need to know.
An Amazing Circus of Phonograms is here today,
And they want to make this fun in every way.
Open your eyes and open your ears
And listen as each phonogram appears!

Before we start our circus show
We have five important guests that you should know.
Each says "**er**" as its sound,
But each has a different spelling we've found.

"er" as in beaver

"ir" as in girl

"ur" as in nurse

"ear" as in pearl

And last of all **(w)**"or" as in worm
Will take its turn.

"er" as in beaver

Veronica Beaver thinks you all deserve
Her wonderful watermelon which she will serve
On paper plates to everyone.
For this super treat let us thank her for a job well done!

"ir" as in girl

Meet Miranda and her twirling pet squirrel.
With her red swirling skirt, Miranda is quite the fashion girl.
Today she brought circus shirts for the whole crowd.
Be the first to get one and cheer out loud
For Miranda, the circus shirt girl
And her lively twirling pet squirrel!

"ur" as in nurse

Our next guest is Ursula who is a very wise nurse.
She is dressed in a coat made of purple furs,
And she carries a medical nurse's purse.
A white nurse cap is the crown she wears,
As she tends your hurts and shows she cares.
Let us give a hand and say, "Hurray!"
For Ursula nurse's visit with us today.

"ear" as in pearl

Earl the Pearl is a shiny young lad,
Who earnestly gave up all that he had
To learn of the earth he had heard so much about.
He searched everywhere and read without doubt.
He has learned and rehearsed many speeches,
And has earned the respect of those whom he teaches.
Now Earl the Pearl gets up early every day.
Give him a hand with a Hip, Hip, Hurray!

(w)"or" _____
Or may say **"er"** when **w** comes before it as in w**or**m.

Worthington
Worm's
Words

Worming his way in is **W**orthington **W**orm who is very bright.
He studies the w**or**ld and reads w**or**ds till late at night.
He doesn't w**or**ry and w**or**ks hard each day.
For his w**or**thy w**or**k he gets no pay.
As he shares his w**or**ld of w**or**ds right now,
Applaud **W**orthington as he takes his bow!

"sh"
The letters **s** and **h** when put together
Share a sound often used by a mother.
"Sh" likes it quiet so it always says "Shhh" to silence the din,
Especially now, since the show is about to begin.

Captain Shark likes to do tricks during his show.
His friend Sherlock Shrimp is ready to go.
When Captain Shark flips his huge tail with a swish,
Sherlock Shrimp soars through the air,
Landing in the shiny round dish.
Shout, "Hurray!" for Captain Shark and friend,
For now their flashy act shall end.

"ee"

Here is the famous performing double **e**
And he says the long sound of the letter **e**
In words such as jeep, tweet, see and queen bee.

BEEP
BEEP

Meet this fantastic eel and bee,
Peewee Lee and Queen Bee Dee!
Around the ring Lee drives his jeep
And honks his horn, "Beep, Beep, Beep."
Queen Bee Dee does a lively reel
Around Peewee Lee's sweet banana peel.
Three cheers for the lively Queen Bee Dee
And for the fantastic eel Peewee Lee!

"th"

When the letters **t** and **h** get together
They have 2 sounds when they work with each other.
The first sound is very soft
As in wealthy, healthy, Beth and Moth.

Here is Beth Ann with her pet Martha Moth,
Who thankfully drinks her thistle broth.
Beth and Martha are extremely healthy.
And both are truly and amazingly wealthy.
Beth washes her pennies in her sudsy bath,
For three thousand pennies Beth Ann hath.
Let us give thirty thumbs up to Beth Ann and her Moth,
And share a cup filled with Martha's healthy thistle broth!

"th"

The second sound tickles your tongue like a feather
As in mother, father, brother and weather.

Welcome Father Bird, who plays the zither.
Mother Bird waters her flowers before they wither.
Brother Bird dons his jacket of leather
Before he goes out into the stormy weather.
Like true birds of a feather they gather together.
They deserve a round of applause like no other!

"ay"
When the letters **a** and **y** play together they like to say
The long sound of the letter **a** as in w**ay**.

The amazing Mayor Blue Jay is here today
From his home so far away,
Balancing upon his head a tray,
While he juggles six balls made of gray clay,
And stands on a small bale of fresh cut hay.
What a talented bird is Mayor Blue Jay.
Now that his act is over he is on his way.
Let us say to the Mayor without delay,
"Hip Hip, Hip Hip, Hip Hip, Hurray!"

"ai"

When the letters **a** and **i** fly together they like to claim
They make the long sound of the letter **a** as in aim.

Meet Daisy Quail with her curly hair.
She flies her airplane in the air.
Daisy comes to entertain with Sailor Snail
Who loves to juggle his pail of nails.
Now clap and shout for this rare pair
Of entertainers from the airplane Fair!

"ow"

When the letters **o** and **w** get together
They have 2 sounds when they work with each other.
Their first sound will make you think
they're hurt when they say "ow"
In words such as owl, clown, towel, and wow.

Mister Brown Owl is a wise old fowl.
His turban is a Turkish towel.
His pet cow Bonnie is dressed like a clown,
And loves to smell the baskets of flowers all over the town.
On Bonnie's head, Owl places a crown.
I ask the crowd to howl and say, "Wow!"
As Bonnie the cow and Mister Brown Owl take a bow.

"ow"

Their second sound is the long sound of the letter o
In words such as grow, sow, bellow and row.

Welcome Lowell to the circus show.
He is a corn grower and wants all of you to know
He sowed his corn seeds in neat little rows,
And kept away the menacing crows
With his fierce looking homemade scarecrow.
Then he picked the corn ears from the stalks high and low,
And gathered them in his own wheelbarrow.
It is time to bellow and shout a big, "Hello!"
For Lowell, the famous corn grower who came to our show!

"ou"

When the letters **o** and **u** march with each other
They make 4 different sounds working together.
Their first sound says "**ow**" as in mouse,
Cloud, ground, countess and house.

The Countess Mouse is here to announce
Her escape from the eagle's attempted pounce.
As he came through the clouds with a mighty bound
She dove into her house in the grassy ground.
This brave Mouse is able to tout
That she was quicker than the eagle, no doubt.
Give a loud shout of praise for Countess Mouse
Who dove for safety in her grassy ground house!

"ou"

Their second sound is the long **o** sound as in four,
Shoulder, poultry, gourd and your.

Courtney Cat is much adored
For on her head she balances a green gourd.
Her shoulders are strong and her arms are too
As she carries a basket of poultry home for her stew.
Now clap your hands four times like that,
Of course, for loveable Courtney Cat!

"ou"
Their third sound is the third sound of the letter **o** as in group,
Coupon, cougar, you and soup.

Louis is a youthful cougar who is very nifty.
He uses his coupons and is very thrifty.
For his hungry cougar group
He purchased seven cases of chicken soup.
Because he used his fifty percent off coupon,
You must cheer this thrifty Louis cougar on!

"ou"

Their fourth sound is like the short sound of the letter **u** as in Double,
Country, cousin, young and trouble.

Douglas and his mischievous country cousin
Keep the curious crowds buzzing.
When they blow their monstrous bubble
Sometimes they can get into trouble.
Now the crowd becomes serious and then "Ka-Boom!"
The bubble explodes all over the room.
Delicious gum balls fall by the dozens.
Let us give a joyous cheer for these famous cousins!

"oa"

When the letters **o** and **a** float in a boat they want you to note
That they say the long sound of **o**
In words such as boat, coal, oatmeal and goat.

Next greet the fearless Toad and Goat
Who went to sea in a huge oak boat.
With a load of chunky blackened coal,
To keep them warm at sea was their goal.
They took loaves of bread made from oats
And all the ingredients for root beer floats.
Send up a roaring cheer for Toad and Goat,
For their fearless voyage in their huge oak boat!

"oy"
When the letters **o** and **y** work together they enjoy
Making the sound as in b**oy**, **oy**ster, and cordur**oy**.

Meet Captain Conroy McCoy
Dressed in a coat made of corduroy.
On his voyages he meets with royalty,
And dines with them and gains their loyalty.
King Leroy and Queen Joyce of Norway
Invited McCoy to a royal lunch one day.
Joyfully they ate soybeans and oysters served on a silver tray.
Clap for joy and shout, "Ahoy!"
To the friendly Captain Conroy McCoy.

"oi"

When the letters **o** and **i** join together in one voice
They make the sound as in noise, coin, and choice.

Joining us this beautiful day
Is the musically talented, Coiya May.
As she sings a song with her angel like voice,
She will broil a sirloin steak of your choice.
Let us throw her gold coins, and with a boisterous noise,
Cheer Coiya May for her excellent poise!

"aw"
When the letters **a** and **w** go walking they obey the phonics law
And make the sound heard in raw, claw, straw and macaw.

Dawson Hawk and Macaw McGraw
Are the most awesome chefs in all of Panama.
With the tasty fruit of the juicy pawpaw
And raw cabbage they make a delicious slaw.
While Macaw McGraw mixes it with his claw,
Dawson Hawk squeezes more juice from the pawpaw
To make a refreshing slushy to drink with a straw.
Squawk and holler with surprise and awe
For Dawson Hawk and Macaw McGraw!

"au"

When the letters **a** and **u** go running they never pause,
But continue to make their sound as in exhaust and cause.

Paul the Auk is a brave and undaunted lad,
Who hauls bags of money to the bank for his Dad.
He is honest and faithful. No fraud would he commit.
Though he may be exhausted, he will never quit.
Now Paul is launching his new banking career,
And was granted the title "Vault Guard of the Year."
For Paul the Auk, lift your voices high,
And applaud and shout praises to the sky!

"ew"
When the letters **e** and **w** work together as a crew
They make the third sound of the letter **o** as in chew.

Here is Newton, who cooks his stew while reading the news,
And on his head he balances his pewter jar of jewels.
His talented nephew juggles a slew of cashews
Along with lots of silver screws.
Let us give a hearty cheer for Newton and nephew,
For here is the newest member of the press crew
Ready to join them for an interview!

"ui"
When letters **u** and **i** sail together they are in pursuit
Of their sound as in juice and fruit.

Tammy Tuna and Petunia Goldfish
Are going on a cruise in a huge copper dish.
Each is wearing a flower colored swimsuit,
And taking a jug of juice and a basket of kiwi fruit.
Tammy and Petunia are in pursuit
Of an island filled with trees of juicy fruit.
Cheer with a holler and give a big whoop
For Tammy Tuna and Petunia Goldfish's fruity pursuit!

When the double **o** performs he is no fool
He has 3 sounds which are pretty cool.
His first sound is like the third sound of letter **o** as in z**oo**
R**oo**ster, n**oo**dles, and bamb**oo**.

ZOO

12:00

Here comes Rooney Rooster who is not a fool.
In his red boots he feels super cool.
At noon Rooney chooses to go to the zoo,
And visit his friends Panda, goose and Kangaroo
They dine on noodles and shoots of bamboo.
This tale is as foolish as a loony cartoon
Join in as we clap and giggle all the way to the moon!

"oo"

The second sound of the double **o** is like the third sound of the letter **u** as in look, brook, soot and nook.

Brooklyn Owl dressed in her hooded coat takes a look
At her books on the shelf in the crooked nook.
There are books about how to cook,
And how to catch a fish on a hook,
How to cut up kindling wood,
And books about how to be good,
Books about running a race barefoot,
And how to clean a chimney full of soot.
Now stomp your foot and give a howl
For the very wise and knowing Brooklyn Owl!

"oo"

The third sound of the double **o** is the long sound of **o** as in floor
Doorbell and door.

OCEAN FLOOR

DOOR JAMB

DOOR STEP

DOOR MAT

Mister Doorman is here today
And has a great deal to say.
"A doorjamb is not what you use to spread on your bread,
But is made up of pieces of board on the sides of a door frame instead.
The ocean floor is not made of floorboards as you may think,
But rocks and sediments of clay that sink.
The doorstep is the step outside the door;
And the doormat is inside the house on the floor.
Now I've said my say and I'll say no more."
Put your feet to the floor and give a mighty roar
For Mister Doorman and his oration on floor and door!

"ch"
When the letters **c** and **h** get together
They make 3 sounds when they work with each other.
Their first sound is in words like sandwich and lunch
Beach, spinach, cheese, chocolate and crunch.

Here are Richard and Chelsea to make us lunch.
They are preparing several things for us to munch.
Chelsea chops spinach and Richard cuts cheese,
And then from the peaches some juice they will squeeze
To make a rich drink to quench our thirst with ease.
Their crunchy chocolate chip cookies always place first,
For they will give your taste buds a chocolate burst.
I ask you all to give a cheer for Richard and Chelsea today
For this munching good lunch they brought our way!

"ch"
Their second sound is like the sound of the letter **k** as in chorus.

Christina is a chemist who will let you know
That the chemical formula for water is H2O.
Christina's hobby is growing lovely chrysanthemums,
And while she tends her flowers happily she hums.
All around her flutter colorful monarch butterflies,
While her pet Chameleon Chloe sings a chorus that echoes to the skies.
Raise your voices in joyous chorus,
And applaud Christina and Chloe as they stand before us!

"ch"

Their third sound is like the sound of **"sh"** as in chef.

Charlene and Michelle live in a Swiss chalet.
Charlene is busy sewing all day,
Making a parachute on her sewing machine,
For parachuting from a plane is her lifelong dream.
Michelle is truly a talented chef supreme.
Her famous dessert is a pistachio cake with whipped cream.
Give a hearty shout for Charlene and Michelle
And praise their talents and dreams as well!

"ea"

When the letters **e** and **a** march together with the beat
They make 3 sounds that are truly neat.
Their first sound says the long sound of the letter **e** as in eat.

Let us welcome the art teacher Jeanie Weasel
Who lives near the beach and eagerly sets up her easel.
She is famous for painting many sea creatures
And many other sea shore features.
Jeanie loves the sunny beach and that is the reason
She lives by the sea during the summer season.
Now clap your hands and give an eager cheer!
From what I hear, Jeanie is the "Art Teacher of the Year!"

"ea"

Their second sound says the short sound of the letter **e** as in bread.

Heather's Healthy Bread

Heather bakes a healthy loaf of bread.
She remembers the whole recipe in her head.
Every ingredient she will carefully measure,
For mixing her bread dough gives her so much pleasure.
To make the bread rise Heather adds the leaven,
And when the bread bakes it smells like heaven.
Heather's bread is now ready and is truly a treasure.
Let us taste a slice and say, "yum," with heavenly pleasure!

"ea"
Their third sound says the long sound of the letter **a** as in gr**ea**t.

Teddy is a great little bear.
He always wears pants that have a tear.
He climbs a tree to pick a pear,
And barbecues steaks and loves to share.
He's bearable and loveable as he will swear.
Break out in applause for this great Teddy bear
Who is huggable and always wants to share!

Author bio

Mary Jo Nyssen was born in South Dakota, but grew up in Salem, Oregon, where she and her husband still live today. As a child, she struggled with reading. After she overcame the challenge, however, she grew to love books and even started writing her own poetry. Though she chose a career in nursing, Nyssen never strayed far from her love of words. As a mother she decided to take a community college class on a multisensory phonics method. After using it to successfully teach her daughters, she soon gained further expertise by helping other children, parents, and teachers.

In 2009, when Nyssen was teaching her preschool-age granddaughter the alphabet, she began creating silly rhymes to make the learning process more fun. These stories became her first book, *A Colorful Journey through the Land of Talking Letters*, and transformed her dream of being an author into a reality.

Made in the USA
San Bernardino, CA
09 August 2015